Rules to Change the World

poems by

Philip Venzke

Finishing Line Press
Georgetown, Kentucky

Rules to Change the World

ACKNOWLEDGMENTS

Bramble: "The Rules for Duck, Duck, Goose"
Harbinger Asylum: "Ther Rules for the Three-Legged Race"
Sheepshead Review: "The Rules for Red Rover"
Shift: A Journal of Literary Oddities: "The Rules for Jacks"
Thunderclap! Magazine: "The Rules For Captain, May I?," "The Rules for
Blindman's Bluff," and "The Rules for Red Light, Green Light"
Vauban, Inc.: "The Rules For Ring Around The Rosy"

Publisher: Leah Huete de Maines
Editor: Christen Kincaid
Cover Art: John Douglas
Author Photo: Susan DeRouchey
Cover Design: Elizabeth Maines McCleavy

Order online: www.finishinglinepress.com
also available on amazon.com

Author inquiries and mail orders:
Finishing Line Press
PO Box 1626
Georgetown, Kentucky 40324
USA

Table of Contents

The Rules For Jacks.. 1

The Rules For Hide-And-Seek.. 2

The Rules For Blindman's Bluff.. 3

The Rules For Keep Away... 4

The Rules For Ring Around The Rosy 5

The Rules For Button, Button—Who's Got The Button?.............. 6

The Rules For Captain, May I?.. 7

The Rules For Hopscotch 8

The Rules For What Time Is It, Mr. Wolf? 9

The Rules For Red Rover 10

The Rules For I Spy... 11

The Rules For The Three-Legged Race 12

The Rules For Simon Says 13

The Rules For Red Light, Green Light 14

The Rules For Capture The Flag 15

The Rules For Musical Chairs 16

The Rules For Duck, Duck, Goose 17

The Rules For Jacks

Scuttle a constellation.

Toss and scatter
the handful of stars.

Bounce the morning sun.
Grab a star before it sets.

Bounce the sun again.
Try for twosies.

And so on until tensies.
The game is now done.

When do we get to play?

The Rules For Hide-And-Seek

First close one eye.
Then close the other.
Peek into yourself

and search every dark corner.
Collect what was lost.
Feel for it in the dark.

When the gathering is done
hide behind your forehead
and let the game begin.

Tell them to find you.
Some will look in the sky.
Some will look in the grass.

They will look for you
in all the places
there are to look.

They will look and look.
And looking for you
they will lose themselves.

The Rules For Blindman's Bluff

Become the blindfold.
Lose your vision.
Because you are it,

your foes will scatter.
But do your best
to catch the rivals.

When you grab one
read the braille
of his lips and nose.

Translate
the sign language
of his eyebrows.

Say his name out loud.
Continue until
the blindfold falls.

The Rules For Keep Away

Find a star.

Bounce the star
under their legs.

Toss the star
over their heads.

If someone catches it
they swallow the star.

Find another star.

Keep playing
until everyone
has swallowed a star.

Become a constellation.

The Rules For Ring Around The Rosy

Stand in a circle.
Hold hands.
Sway back and forth.

Begin to hum
until the ring
spins so fast
it lifts into the sky.

As it nears the sun
it whirls into a rose
and fades away.

There is no ash.

We don't fall down.

The Rules For Button, Button—Who's Got The Button?

Stand in a circle.
Hold your hands out.
Put your palms together.

The button holds a secret.
It back-slaps
as it travels around the circle.

When your hand is shaken,
it passes you the secret.

It is your turn to guess.
You can't lose.

Everyone believes
they have the secret.

The Rules For Captain, May I?

First, go to sea.
Then become a captain.
Sail to the end of the world.

Anchor your ship at the edge.
Don't let it slide into the abyss.

Call out loudly over the water:
"Take three very fluid steps."

Wait for an answer.
If only seaweed responds,
there is no hope.

The Rules for Hopscotch

Your design will vary
from what they expect.

And you decide
what is home
and what is safe.

The game starts
when you toss stars
onto the squares.

And as you skip
past the stars,
you eat them.

You play
throughout the night.
In the morning
you are a galaxy.

The Rules for What Time Is It, Mr. Wolf?

Mr. Wolf crouches
with his back toward the foes.

The foes ask in unison:
"What time is it Mr. Wolf?"

Mr. Wolf answers with a time:
"It is midnight."

The foes race toward Mr. Wolf
and shout in unison:
"What time is it Mr. Wolf?"

Mr. Wolf turns
and whispers through his teeth:
"It is supper time."

The Rules for Red Rover

First, divide yourself in two.
Hold arms.
Make sure you don't let go.

Call out to your foe
in your two new voices
and brace yourself for the blow.

Just before the hit
become one again.

Enjoy watching the pieces
roll away.

Pick them up
and add them to yourself.

Now, divide yourself three ways.
Call out to your foe.
Again.

The Rules for I Spy

I see, I see
what you don't see.

I hear, I hear
what you don't hear.

I taste, I taste
what you don't taste.

I smell, I smell
what you don't smell.

I feel, I feel
what you don't feel.

I spy, I spy
what you don't spy.

The Rules for The Three-Legged Race

Find your enemy.

Bind your left leg
to his right leg.

Turn each other's
bones to marbles.

Now the race can start.

Hop and hop and hop
toward the finish line.

Marbles cascade to the ground.

When will a winner
be announced.

The Rules for Simon Says

Simon says hold your sides
so when you laugh
your sides won't burst.

You hold and hold
and find you have no sides.

Simon says wipe your brow
so when you sweat
your eyes won't sting.

You reach to wipe.
You have no brow.

Simon says hands on chest
so your heart won't leap
and bounce away.

You reach to cover.
You have no chest.

You are only hands.
Turn palms up
so they catch the rain.

Simon says
and grass begins to grow.

The Rules for Red Light, Green Light

Make sure you have no front.
Make sure you are all back.
They will know you are it.

Sense your foes sneaking up on you.
Remember to keep your back to them.

As they near, become a traffic light.
Click your signal to red.
Your foes will freeze.

Use all your clout.
Hold that signal red.

When every foe is frozen,
call out to the sun:
"go away, go far, far away."

The Rules for Capture The Flag

Acquire a taste
for wind.

Pour that breeze
into a chalice.
Look at its clarity.
Watch how it swirls.

Smell the gale.
Infect your sinuses.
Tickle your nostrils.

Start with a small sip.
Let the draft twist
around your tongue.

Let your tongue
whip in the gust.

Dare people
to steal it.

The Rules for Musical Chairs

Slide up to the lonely chair.
Wait for the music to begin.

Hold the chair tight.
Firm hand to the back.

Under the cover of music
whisper into its ear.

Dip the chair slightly
until it begins to sigh.

Along the wall, the chairs
stare and cluck their tongues.

Cluck, cluck, cluck.
Until their tongues

fall out.

The Rules for Duck, Duck, Goose

Enter the circle
without being seen.

Duck down low.

If you are touched,
become a feather.

Toss yourself
into the wind.

Search for other feathers.

Talk with them.
Become a wing.

Circle back to the game.

Philip Venzke grew up on a dairy farm near Colby, Wisconsin. A lifelong student of creative writing, he graduated from the University of Wisconsin at Stevens Point under the nurturing guidance and mentorship of Richard Behm and Larry Watson. After moving to Cedarburg, Philip married his UWSP college sweetheart, Susan DeRouchey.

Accepted into MFA Programs in Creative Writing at University of Oregon, University of Montana, and State University of New York (SUNY), Venzke choose instead to serve his country, enlisting with the U.S. Navy. He completed two Pacific tours of duty in the North Arabian Sea and Persian Gulf, while home-ported in Alameda, CA, and received numerous decorations for his service. After military service, Venzke worked in the Information Technology (IT) world until his recent retirement.

Venzke's poetry and translations have been published extensively in the U.S. and abroad. His first chapbook of poetry, "Chant to Save the World", was a prize winner in SurVision Book's 4th annual James Tate International Poetry Contest in Ireland. His poetry can also be found in "Contemporary Surrealist and Magical Realist Poetry" (An International Anthology) published in December 2022 by Lamar University Press. "Rules to Change the World" is his second chapbook of poetry.

A continuing love of world travel invigorates him, providing inspiration, education and enlightenment rarely found elsewhere. His travels have included destinations in Africa, Australia, Asia and Europe. When not planning his next terrestrial adventure, Venzke is a creative cook and avid zymurgist. He and his wife, Susan, reside in Wisconsin.

www.ingramcontent.com/pod-product-compliance
Lightning Source LLC
Chambersburg PA
CBHW022110080426
42734CB00009B/1548